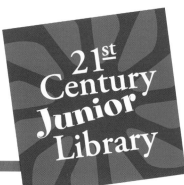

21st
Century
Junior
Library

Pterosaur

by Jennifer Zeiger

CHERRY LAKE PUBLISHING * ANN ARBOR, MICHIGAN

Published in the United States of America by Cherry Lake Publishing
Ann Arbor, Michigan
www.cherrylakepublishing.com

Content Adviser: Gregory M. Erickson, PhD, Paleontologist, Department of Biological Science,
Florida State University, Tallahassee, Florida

Reading Adviser: Marla Conn, Read With Me Now

Photo Credits: Cover and page 8, © Elenarts/Shutterstock.com; pages 4 and 10, © Linda Bucklin/
Shutterstock.com; page 6, © Catmando/Shutterstock.com; page 12, © Michael Rosskothen/
Shutterstock.com; page 14, © Photobank gallery/Shutterstock.com; page 16, © leonello calvetti/
Shutterstock.com; page 18, © Ozja/Shutterstock.com; page 20, © Natural Visions/Alamy.

LIBRARY OF CONGRESS CATALOGING-IN-PUBLICATION DATA
Zeiger, Jennifer, author.
  Pterosaur / by Jennifer Zeiger.
      pages cm.—(Dinosaurs) (21st century junior library)
  Summary: "Learn all about the ancient animals known as Pterosaurs, from where they lived to how
they hunted for food."—Provided by publisher.
  Audience: K to grade 3
  Includes bibliographical references and index.
  ISBN 978-1-63362-385-9 (lib. bdg.)—ISBN 978-1-63362-413-9 (pbk.)—
ISBN 978-1-63362-441-2 (pdf)—ISBN 978-1-63362-469-6 (e-book)
  1. Pterosauria—Juvenile literature. I. Title.
QE862.P7Z45 2016
567.918—dc23   2014045658

*Cherry Lake Publishing would like to acknowledge the work of
The Partnership for 21st Century Skills.
Please visit www.p21.org for more information.*

Printed in the United States of America
Corporate Graphics
July 2015

CONTENTS

A pterosaur flies through the sky, looking for food.

What Was a Pterosaur?

An animal soars high over the heads of dinosaurs. Its long wings flap once. It **glides** out over the ocean. Suddenly, it swoops down! The animal's long beak reaches into the water. It comes up holding a flapping fish. Is this hunter a bird? A dinosaur? Nope. It's a pterosaur!

Giant sauropod dinosaurs, such as the titanosaur,
lived at the same time as pterosaurs.

Pterosaurs were flying **reptiles**. They were not dinosaurs. But they were around at the same time as dinosaurs. Pterosaurs lived between 228 million and 66 million years ago. They were found around the world. You will not see any living pterosaurs now, though. They are **extinct**.

Look!

Look at a picture of a pterosaur. Then look up pictures of reptiles that live today. You can find images in books or online. What does a pterosaur have in common with today's reptiles? How is it different?

This pterosaur has a long, pointed crest on its head.

What Did a Pterosaur Look Like?

Most pterosaurs had short bodies. They had long necks and beaks. Many had head **crests**. Some pterosaurs had tails. Others had no tail at all. Their back legs were long and thin like a bird's. Their feet had sharp, curved claws. Pterosaurs had no feathers. Some had something similar to hair. This may have kept them warm.

Pterosaur means "winged lizard."

A pterosaur's wings looked like bat wings. They had bare skin. One part of each wing connected to the reptile's body. The other part stretched along the arm to the tip of a very long finger. When a pterosaur stuck its arms out, its wings stretched out.

Make a Guess!

Pterosaurs needed strong arms. Can you guess why? To help you figure it out, try moving. Stick your arms straight out to the sides. How long can you hold them up? Now flap your arms. Are you getting tired?

The largest pterosaurs were larger than any of today's birds.

Different kinds of pterosaurs were different sizes. Some were as small as sparrows. Others were much bigger. The largest had wings that stretched more than 36 feet (11 meters) across. It was the largest flying animal ever.

When gliding, a pterosaur would not flap its wings much.

How Did a Pterosaur Live?

Experts think small pterosaurs flapped their wings to fly. Bigger pterosaurs usually glided. On land, pterosaurs probably walked on all four feet.

An animal must be lightweight to fly. Bones are heavy. Today's birds have light, hollow bones. Pterosaurs also had hollow bones. They were about as thick as a few pages of paper!

15

Sharp teeth helped some pterosaurs catch prey.

Pterosaurs were **predators**. They ate meat. Pterosaurs had very good eyesight. They could spot **prey** while flying high above.

Some pterosaurs lived near the water. They probably ate fish and other water animals. There were also pterosaurs that ate bugs and other small land animals. The largest pterosaurs may have eaten dead animals, including dinosaurs.

The shape of this pterosaur's beak may have
helped the animal crack open sea animals' shells.

Some pterosaurs had short, sharp teeth. They could grip slippery fish or other prey. Other pterosaurs had long, thin teeth. These predators could grab mouthfuls of water with sea animals in it. The water flowed out between the pterosaurs' teeth. The sea animals stayed inside the predator's mouth. Some pterosaurs had no teeth. Experts think they swallowed fish whole. This is what pelicans do today.

Some lucky fossil finds include most of a pterosaur's bones.

We know about pterosaurs from **fossils**. The first pterosaur fossil was found in 1784. Since then, many more have been found. Some fossils are bones. Others are footprints or other remains. Each new fossil holds clues to how these animals lived. There is always more to learn. Someday you could make pterosaur discoveries!

Ask Questions!

What can a person learn from old bones and footprints? Talk to a parent, teacher, or librarian about it. Do they know? Ask them to help you look for the answers. You can search in books or online.

GLOSSARY

crests (KRESTS) bumps on animals' skulls formed by bone or tufts of feathers, fur, or skin

extinct (ek-STINGKT) describing a type of plant or animal that has completely died out

fossils (FAH-suhlz) the preserved remains of living things from thousands or millions of years ago

glides (GLIDEZ) flies without flapping wings

predators (PRED-uh-turz) animals that live by hunting other animals for food

prey (PRAY) an animal that is hunted by other animals for food

reptiles (REP-tilez) cold-blooded, scaly animals that usually reproduce by laying eggs

FIND OUT MORE

BOOKS

Nunn, Daniel. *Pterodactyl*. Chicago: Heinemann Library, 2015.

Riggs, Kate. *Pterodactyls*. Mankato, MN: Creative Education, 2012.

WEB SITES

American Museum of Natural History— Pterosaurs: Flight in the Age of Dinosaurs

www.amnh.org/exhibitions/past -exhibitions/pterosaurs-flight-in-the-age -of-dinosaurs
Watch videos about pterosaurs and listen to experts talk about these ancient animals.

BBC Nature—Prehistoric Life: Pterosaurs

www.bbc.co.uk/nature/life /Pterosaur
Check out videos about pterosaurs and their relatives.

INDEX

ABOUT THE AUTHOR

Jennifer Zeiger lives in Chicago, Illinois. She writes and edits children's books on all sorts of topics.